DAVID A. BROWN / DABFOTO CREATIVE

ANGE MLINKO

MARVELOUS THINGS OVERHEARD

Ange Mlinko was born in Philadelphia in 1969. Educated at St. John's College and Brown University, she lived in New York for many years and has also spent time in Ifrane, Morocco, and Beirut, Lebanon. Her previous books include *Matinées, Starred Wire,* and *Shoulder Season.* She is the recipient of a 2014 Guggenheim Fellowship and the Poetry Foundation's Randall Jarrell Award in Criticism, and she teaches in the University of Houston's Creative Writing Program. She lives in Houston, Texas, with her husband and two children.

MARVELOUS

THINGS

OVERHEARD

FARRAR STRAUS GIROUX / NEW YORK

MARVELOUS

THINGS

OVERHEARD

ANGE MLINKO

Farrar, Straus and Giroux
18 West 18th Street, New York 10011

Published in 2013 by Farrar, Straus and Giroux
First paperback edition, 2014

The Library of Congress has cataloged the hardcover edition as follows:
Mlinko, Ange.
   [Poems. Selections]
   Marvelous things overheard / Ange Mlinko. — First edition.
   pages ; cm.
   ISBN 978-0-374-20314-6
   I. Title.

PS3563.L58 M27 2013
811'.54—dc23

                                        2013006489

ISBN: 978-0-374-53480-6

Designed by Quemadura

Farrar, Straus and Giroux books may be purchased for
educational, business, or promotional use. For information
on bulk purchases, please contact the Macmillan Corporate
and Premium Sales Department at 1-800-221-7945,
extension 5442, or write to specialmarkets@macmillan.com.

www.fsgbooks.com
www.twitter.com/fsgbooks
www.facebook.com/fsgbooks

P1

TO STEVE, JAKE, AND GRAY, WITH ALL LOVE

The she-goats in Cephallenia do not drink, as it appears,
like other quadrupeds; but daily turning their faces towards
the sea, open their mouths, and take in the breezes.

ARISTOTLE, *On Marvelous Things Heard*

CONTENTS

III

I

THE GRIND

Three ciabbatini for breakfast
where demand for persnickety bread
is small, hence its expense, hence my steadfast
recalculation of my overhead,

which soars, and as you might expect
the ciabbatini stand in for my fantasy
of myself in a sea-limned prospect,
on a terrace, with a lemon tree . . .

Not: Assessed a fee for rent sent a day late.
Not: Fines accrued for a lost library book.
Better never lose track of the date.
Oversleep, and you're on the hook.

It's the margin for error: shrinking.
It's life ground down to recurrence.
It's fewer books read for the thinking
the hospital didn't rebill the insurance;

the school misplaced the kids' paperwork.
Here's our sweet pup, a rescue
which we nonetheless paid for, and look:
he gets more grooming than I do.

When I turn my hand mill, I think of the dowager
who ground gems on ham for her guests;
the queen who ground out two cups of flour
on the pregnant abdomen of her husband's mistress;

I think of a great "rock-eating bird"
grinding out a sandy beach,
the foam said to be particulate matter
of minute crustaceans, each

brilliantly spooning up Aphrodite
to Greek porticoes, and our potatoes,
and plain living which might be
shaken by infinitesimal tattoos.

WORDS ARE THE REVERSE OF PAIN

Had something gone wrong then I wouldn't be here
to tell you this: In November 1944 a baby boy was born
in Germany—"in a cave," they kept saying,
"she gave birth in a cave."
The villages between Minsk and Hannover
—untold dozens of them—zigzagged through,
one child on her back, another under her heart.
From the distance of the bombers,
she might have looked like she was dancing.

Who thinks a woman in labor might be dancing?
From a distance of gods, Leto might have been dancing,
the Leto whom Hera hated. The Leto who reeled
in search of a place to give birth. Fled Arcadia, Leto did.
Fled Parthenium, fled the land of Pelops,
fled Aonia too and Dirce and Strophia.
From such a distance it might have looked like a dance
as she tottered from city to city to city,
none letting her rest in their precincts.
None letting her loosen her elastic-panel
drawstring jeans.

Leto island-hopped. They would not let the baby drop,
not the Echinades of the famously welcoming harbor,

not the normally hospitable Corcyra, not Cos.
It can seem so cordial, this sea, with its views
clear to spiky urchins fifty feet below. And the islands
close but uncrowded, like cousins slumped about
on pillows waiting for an adored movie to begin.
Think of Leto groaning amid them—trying to sweat a pearl.
Think of us cousins, watching Rudolph on Christmas Eve,
so many years after the camps and the ruses—
lifetimes ago—pretending to be Polish!

The villages between Minsk and Hannover
—untold dozens of them—zigzagged through,
one child on her back, another under her heart.
From the distance of the bombers,
she might have looked like she was playing hide-and-seek.

There was an island not permitted to anchor,
named Asteria. Asteria wandered
across the Aegean, across the Saronic Gulf
until some unnamed wind blew that midwife,
part earth part skiff, and Leto together.
The island took pity, and let Leto deliver.
Hera couldn't intervene. Asteria had once been a woman
who accepted punishment rather than bed Zeus.
Double bind rebounded.
After succoring Leto, the island could anchor at last.
She became renowned as the heart of the Cyclades, Delos.

Why do we have to know this? That cruelty
has to exist to propel kindness into relief; that relief
must first imply pain? They said this was the turning point.
That her health was never the same.
Giving birth in a cave, on the frozen plain of Germany.
So it's ironic that Leto's jammed labor would yield a god
in whose presence it is forbidden to cry.
Did you know? Apollo! Arrester of tears.
A god in whose presence it is impossible to grieve.
Application of the tender to the elemental:
my thumb stops the knife's turn through a carrot.
A dog roughs his tongue lapping rain on cement.
A callus rises. But words? Words are the reverse of pain.
Where pain is, no words are. Apollo loves words.

THE GOD CATEGORY

1. FLASHFLOOD: ARETHUSA

The vibration running through the ebbing afternoon
isn't unusual. The wind is.
The direction of bent boughs
gives it away: All flags,
all fealty follows our sirocco, our feral
anti-zephyr, west.
Now they say the maiden spotted in the light
that bleeds through pine and oak and gravy moss
(it drips) was ankle-deep in
swamp violets when she
cried out to the goddess.
Oh, aid me! —
me, *me*, 'til all *m* was was wave. The exulting god
foamed, went after her, you know the way
the trickle of a levee
overcome by a storm surge
bucks furiously against
concrete retaining walls
and thrashes toward the culvert?
The shape of a freshwater spring
shot into the sea from an
underground grotto

was Arethusa fleeing
(see thermal imaging)
and the god in pursuit. Hence
rumors of underwater plumes,
grue and violet, that savagely
fluoresce offshore.

2. SQUALL: ECHO

Now, what if Echo came to their shores—somewhere between
    Westport and New Rochelle,
and made herself a paperweight on one of those overwrought
    wicker chairs
the wind could pulp to papyrus starter—
and holding a stem of chardonnay, eavesdropped on party
    chatter by the mod wok
before wandering on in search of her old suitor?

What we need is a suitor perpetually new, the wives agreed
    (their imported spreads, their filigreed eyelids).
What we need are marvelous things, they said, but Echo
    could not say what *she* had seen.
Sitting among their pale accessories, all in harmony with white
    ceramic tile,
eggshell balcony railings, green-grape sunlight spilling on the
    metallurgical sound of the waves—more like staves—
    collapsing,
and so collapsing every riff into one note.

The sand was all one color, oat, and the grasses kept
    rebearding where hosanna-ing thalassas
massacred oysters to pure nacre.

I have seen some things, she opened her mouth to say (this
　　could have been anywhere: Tyre, Florida; Essouaira,
　　California; Texel, Massachusetts).
I have seen marvelous things, akin to shine on a child's straight
　　hair or brushed titanium
of the early adopter's new trophy.

These things, against what they obsolesce
do not make us feel less less,

they implied, giving Echo a severe look.
Echo wound a tress around her finger; they had all looked up at
　　comets through telescopes and at the ceiling of
　　Grand Central, when it came down to it;
Shakespeare in the Park, with actors previously seen onscreen;
traveled, raveled, veiled and led on donkeys through casbahs.
They were like poems conceived, typical poems, near the
　　metronome;
they preferred common complaints.
Good riddance to the husband who put the steak knives point-up
like myrmidons in the dishwasher.
And if in their co-ops in Westport, or New Rochelle, or
　　wherever, they resembled, a little, pigeons—"Djinns,"
Echo flattered them, making them feel less less, but somehow
　　not all that appreciated for it,
as when she had whispered to Narcissus "Us!" rather than, as
　　he would have had it, "Scissor us."

3. TORNADO: ARACHNE

Do you remember who it was Arachne offended
when she wove her fateful tapestry?

It was the goddess whose handiwork organizes
the transient fabric of tornadoes,
wedding tulle of broken homes
(exploded foam and particleboard).
One intrepid plane penetrates a chink
and drops a hundred golf balls in the vortex,
each equipped with sensors that relay
measurements back to the lab.
By these criteria, the rainbow,
statistically difficult to verify,
gets classified as pure illusion.

And so love. Even in the city,
which seemed to offer protection
from disaster sweeping in from the prairie,
we were alerted to the funnels
the spinning goddess wrought, a displeasure
like the one she unleashed on Arachne,
who had depicted Zeus's adultery

(the goddess was, of course, his daughter).
Who would agree to a tapestry contest
with a weaver of weather?
I mix up Arachne with Ariadne:
similar name, similar gesture—
the string flung from her spinneret sleeve
and given in trust to a lover, who dropped down
bravely into another family's entanglements.

4. HURRICANE: HERA

You never hear of Ixion, tied to a revolving wheel,
but it's an axiom that, sooner or later, a hurricane'll hit here.
The art students made a map of the one-hundred-year flood
    plain superimposed on the five-hundred-year flood
    plain
and you were supposed to stick a thumbtack on the street
    where you were living in the prequel, shaded a blue so
    appealing
it seemed as though we might have taken nutriment from it,
    with some organ we have lost.

The art students were making their installation serve a religious
    function
by offering an opportunity for communal expression.
Catharsis.
Should we choose to participate, the result would belong to all
    of us.

The ironclad customs that once proclaimed the common good
    are vanished completely
but in the sanctuary city, just as in ancient times, people ask
    the gods a question in prayer and sleep on it.

When Ixion raped a Hera-shaped cloud, it produced the father
    of a new race, the Centaurs, whose specialty was
    medicine.

The medical center is like a palace complex.
The live oaks knit their limbs in prayerlike attitudes that
    mimic, altogether, the vault of a cathedral.
I would ask the art students what kind of knowledge it would
    take to be able to paint a tortured body—
Christ in his passion, Ixion on his wheel. I can see them recoil.
Some kinds of knowledge are hateful, as the nuclear scientist,
    assassinated, will tell you,
or a Dutch gentlewoman who is so traumatized
when her husband buys an uncanny Ixion by the artist Ribera
that she gives birth to a child whose hand is withered and
    twisted—as though pain
could be born of paint.

STABILE

I wake to light jackhammering, and news
follows: a plane
failed over the sea. All want to go home, but drastic curfews
obtain from a meridian.

●

We are a long way from a sea that cedes
black boxes from an area
forested like the Andes. Instead, a Mercedes,
black as La Brea,

leaps from the backlit red, anonymous,
when we try to cross
at the traffic island discarding hibiscus
with every wind-toss.

●

We are a long way from the courteous lilac
or waxwing
with sensitive feather tipped as a kayak
is tipped by a coxswain.

THE HELIOPOLITAN

"But the Romans must have built this *here* for a reason,"
he exclaimed. He was Jean Cocteau! Rain fell on the ruins
as he drew in his sketch pad the rooster with a *toe*.

"There are for instance," he instructed, "spots on the earth
where gravity is so light it barely exerts a *pull*."
He lightly clucked as the pencil ran about. "Pillars!

Like these! Do you imagine they moved themselves?"
"It's also unusual to be raining here," another guest remarked.
The owner of the Palmyra saw to us himself.

In the dim room the gold in the throw pillows
and tasseled pull cords glitt-*air*ed. "*Heurtebise*,"
he said of me, tipping my chin: "*L'ange Heurtebise*."

And there where the mules were banked against the rain,
we heard the story of ____ the Flaccid
who sacked the temple of Hera and disturbed her cattle,

and not cattle only but the silver trees, and the hitherto
unstirred ashes on the altar. So when the *redemptores*
brought back the tiles of the roof ____ the Flaccid dismantled,

it was by vote of the Senate; for the idea of leaving roofless
even that humble shrine (humble, that is, compared
to the uses to which they could have put that marble in Rome)

left them terribly terribly uneasy, perhaps because
_____ the Flaccid had since then lost his mind.
Do not lift a single tile, a single tessera, not a potsherd,

they laughed; but our hero kept his eye on his sketch pad.
"How easy it was to put treacherous beacons on the shoals;
steal a map; distribute counterfeit maps;

falsify navigational charts, or the names for things
in foreign languages." As a rhododactyl turns the page
tonight I blurted, "It stopped raining."

Then the man who said, "*Etonnez-moi!*"
and walked through a mirror
awarded his *coq* with its big toe to the proprietor.

NEO-AEOLIAN

"Next time," I heard the old one say,

"they want to throw a new wind my way,

for inclusion in the illustrious bag,

twinning the wind from a propeller

with the *mistral* or the *levanter*

along with the lesser breezes

from the electric fan and HVAC vent,

the wind from freeways

being all the same to them

as that which jittered palm trees

way back when

let them wake on the dawn side of an Airbus

to see a smaller plane go haywire

in those jazzy 'wingtip vortices'

and if that doesn't tap their fear of Erebus

show them what it'll do to a lyre

whose delicate artifices

hold up their lives like an eyelid's

unseen caryatid."

ALEXANDER'S NAMING OF THE WINDS

If you'd seen
    lightning nets in clear water,
midnight blue beyond the reefs;
    the pattern intact on nippled juglets;
if you'd seen
    feral cats dozing on jagged steles when the noon sun
drugged us
    you'd say too, *Can't I have it*—
Or if I could describe it,
    I could have it? Like an ancient contest?
They say Apeliotes
    is called Potameus here in Phoenicia;
between the mountains
    of Libanus
and Bapyrus it blows from a plain like a vast threshing floor;
    it might also be called Syriandus in the Gulf of Issus,
which blows from the Syrian Gates
    between the Rosian Mountains
and the Taurus.
    In Tripoli they call it Marseus.
On the border of Syria,
    the southeast wind, the Eurus, is called Scopeleus,
but in Cyrene
    it is known as Phoenicias. I can't have this.

But they say
　　these Phoenicians
who sailed to the Pillars of Hercules
　　with oil to trade
came back with more silver than they could carry
　　and were forced to refit their ship's wheel,
keel, and anchors
　　with silver,
not to mention their tableware,
　　cookware, and fixtures.
And though they say the Phoenicians received their name
　　from the Greek *phoenixai*,
"to stain with blood," because they slew
　　and murdered
as they streamed over the sea,
　　if you'd seen the murex pits,
the very waves disperpling the shore with the dye of the snail,
　　you'd know what those kingdoms were stained with.
I can have it;
　　describe it thus;
and though no one can claim "this wind
　　is the wind of the palace,"
we must hope for the Leuconotus,
　　the white wind,
to arrive from the south if the Potameus
　　or Syriandus

or Marseus or Phoenicias
    won't come to our aid—no wind is the king's—
but if you'd seen,
    as I saw,
at the fundus of the world,
    snakes desquamate their own simulacra;
eggs shiver at a tambourine;
    a Eurydice
essay toward the nest;
    for good measure, not to lose the contest,
you would pray for a wind to come,
    the rough marine roof
kicked up by the hoof of Notus if necessary,
    its bad air
notwithstanding, to bear you back to where the language
    bore its auger into ears of matching description,
though it cause great storms
    in the harbor at Posidonium.

ETNA

She wakes at dawn. Eos has played some kind of trick:
all is covered in ash. As if she were in some old flick.

DUTCH

Bashing the butt end of a broomstick on my eye
I was in luck: the contact lens fell right out in my hand.
    Sitting down, nursing my eye,
I let my son put in the disk of Sister Wendy
discussing a Dutch painting
with a man, a couple of women, and a coin in it.
The coin is the tip-off that this is a brothel.
I must pause and decide whether a six-year-old boy
should be watching a nun elucidate
a four-hundred-year-old painting on the sale of flesh.

On account of Omar Pasha's elegant handwriting,
the governorship of this port city fell to him.
    His household women made soap.
The dissolving escutcheons released such perfume,
his musicians ran through "Ah! Che la morte,"
and his plans for desalinization
included a vast cistern under the tennis court.
That we're on this headland, surrounded by water,
makes atmospheric tricks; worlds in an optical inch.
It's spring and it's windy. Even my ears unsynch.

CIVILIZATION

The Venetians, the Venetians—
    you hear about the Venetians
picking off the black grapes of Izmir
    or seizing a ship
bound for Egypt, to trigger a
    war for Crete; grabbing the wrong rein
in the king's convoy, causing riots;
    leaving their powder in the
Parthenon, to explode and singe
    the ancient trees to extinction
along with the friezes and free-
    standing tibias of Phidias
and Praxiteles. So when a
    ruddy dove, as if burnt by sunset,
staggers onto the balcony
    on the day the tripped munitions
kill more than a dozen
    and destroy a power plant
months after being intercepted
    on a ship bound for a Syrian port,

the first thing I think is
    "The Venetians! The Venetians!"
collapsing the shelves
    while olive silvers . . .

II.

The Dutch called their money florins,
    and their borrowed flora,
which didn't smell, made money.
    They didn't smell,
those tulips from the east.
    The east,
      whose aitches and hitches—
an "a'a" like "raw almond"—
    alternated
like the arabesques in *assassins.*
    The Dutch were so proud
of their invincible navy ships
    and varieties of tulips
that, crossing "Virgin"
    with "Admiral van Enckhuysen"
or "Diana" with "Semper Augustus,"
    they bred, by and by,
    "General Bol" and "Admiral van Hoorn"
and sent their waves
    on tiptoe.

THE MED

If there were a way to set it right,
because life, for all its shortcomings,
Aimée, is a resource not to be squandered
on desire for the impossible,
or love for that which is absent,
then Cheiron would know it, the Centaur,
who, roaming the meadows of Pelion,
knew every herb and its medicinal properties,
in one of the most florid
ecological systems in the world,
such that every island
in the Aegean archipelago
might contain plants indigenous to it
and found nowhere else, not even on the next island;
so I, raceme of pleasure, imagine the wind
as the instrument of justice, scattering memes
on territory unknown and stymied,
hostile to fennel—striving
to bless Pelion with diverse spore.
Cheiron, who raised Apollo's infant
to be the god of healing after his mother was obliterated
for straying, that is, loving what was far away,
impossible, or absent—

(ahem, Aimée) no doubt Cheiron
researched a remedy for that.
But consider a worse fate, my dear:
Consider a ballerina
who dances a benefit for her choreographer
as the villain Polio; she pretends to fall, stricken;
but gold ingots, tossed at her by a ring of children,
heal her miraculously;
a dozen years later polio, for real,
cuts her at the waist.

Cheiron might have had a remedy
among the pollen
and we have one too. It's much more essential
than what's required to heal so light a loss as love,
which we don't have. (The ballerina married, Aimée,
the maestro who played Polio.)
So, however powerful the indifference
of beautiful men,
remember this, and think instead
of Marie Taglioni: To remind herself
of the night she danced
on a panther skin on the snow, beneath the stars,
for a stranger,
a highwayman who'd waylaid her,
she watched an ice cube dissolve in her jewel box.
In the museum where we saw it, Aimée, it glows

the color of the sea near certain villages where fall
the narrow blades of shadow rudders
pointing to bedrooms
darkened at midday;
the sea is violet with iodine.

SYMPHONIC EXPANSE

If you'd seen
the Gaillardots' mullein in the cedars of Al-Shouf;
if you'd seen the Aleppo dock, russet with iron,
in Bsharre where the Adonis River's said to run as red

with what was
thought his blood; if you'd seen the bearded oat in Burjein,
the rayed white horehound in Tripoli; or maybe
the milkwort in Ehden, as often I saw the strigose bellflower

and the cyclamen,
you might have been the more awed by a mallow-leaved
bindweed in Aley on your way to the brunnera in Baalbek.
The Mediterranean poppy in Nabatieh, Beirut mullein

in nearby Baabda,
connate alexanders in Qadisha, fodder vetch in Zgharta,
white rocket in Sour, gypsywort in Marjeyoun,
headed ziziphora in Baakleen, bladder skullcap in Barouk.

The viscid catchfly,
ah, vying with bats at evening in Zahle—for these the earth
of continuous habitation since the Chalcolithic Age
salivates at dawn. But not a reed grows where no grave is.

In Sacandaga Valley,
two thousand bodies were trans-buried by the boneyard gang.
They ceded the pitted ground to the dentist gang,
whose jackhammers drilled the rock beneath.

Powder monkeys tamped
the holes with dynamite. The beaver-tooth gang's axes
and cross-cut saws cleared the trees. Bush burners followed.
The fires burned for two years. The patience of dam-builders

built a force
to equal the water: It flooded the ashes, the station,
and a train, which I saw transposed in the steely swells,
or so it seemed. But iron turns a torrent red.

NAIAD MATH

You should see us try to fix numbers on our slates.
Not the cuneiform weapons of swordfish could aid us

when rounding off near an estuary.
Doing arithmetic, we turn color like the octopus.

Geometry is just as difficult—adding aquaeous angles
during rough winds made one of the Limnades weep.

(We weep anyway, by our hems and hair ends.)
But counting spirals and stripes on shelly things delights us:

noticing series voiced by cicadas, likewise.
There's solace in the horizon: the nothingness above

divided by this teemingness below
makes room, by which we come to figure.

•

The *continuum assumption* states that we
are none of us discrete, but move in kind

through your cerebrum, without which
there would be no medium for thinking.

And yet they flow through you sparkling,
these mental waters, only at our discretion.

A three-dimensional vortex begins to rotate
and comes the wave cascading on itself

flexing like the flank of the oryx as it runs;
flushing the pipes and mouths the years

have fashioned from habitual assumption
like glimmering variables through an algorithm.

CICADAS

Gray rainbows in the nighttime irrigation.
Immediately forgotten.
Then I hear a child carry a tune in a whisper.

I was dashing through those ashen rainbows
immediately forgotten.
You could truncate butterfly to butte

and still get migration and a cumin route.
But not camel.
Not emu. Not Tuareg. Not a Russian garlic

dome like painted clove on steppe nor geodesic
ostrich egg.
Totally forgotten, 'til the child's moonbow tune

whispered in what wagon, rickshaw, landau
rattled me to a carrefour.
I couldn't tell the autumn from the drought,

crescent over Quonset hut, or put language
to the pulp that made me ill.
Inside the mouth of the water-flow monitors,

goblin goblin—robin. New World cicadas
that chant in parabolas.
A new address—a dryness—they stop. A focal chill.

BAYT

1. LABID'S ''LAST SIMILE''

It's as if she were an *earn*,

        gebideo prey for her eyrie.

Perched alertly,

        a *hægtesse* on their innards.

In bitter *morgenceald*,

        her hoar-glittered feathers.

Suddenly she sees

        a fox on the *westen*.

At that she rouses,

        heaved up on high,

and heads straight at him,

        in harrowing *hæste*.

Hearing her, he freezes

        his tail. He's terrified.

Sees, *stela*,

               with *eagfleah* flashing,

talons overtake him,

               dash him down in torment,

overtake him again,

               sweng him on the *eorde*.

One yelp as she pincers his liver.

               Wyrd—pierces aorta.

We wither, unlike stars;

                  die, unlike hills and cisterns.

Ana shadowed my protector,

                  esteemed Arbad, who's left us.

But *ana* do not grieve;

                  all sparrows exit the feast hall.

Novelties don't excite me,

                  nor does *wyrdstaef* affright me.

Men are like encampments

                  that soon become ruins.

They come with their kin,

                  leave only land behind them when
                      they go—

the last herdsman

                  rounding up the stragglers.

Man's a shooting star:

                    light turned to ash.

Wealth and kin a stain

                    that eventually wears off.

The work we do

                    inevitably *gehrorene*.

The wise grasp this;

                    the foolish fight and lose.

If my *wyrd* holds off awhile,

                    my fingers reach out for its stick.

Ana can tell you stories,

                    bent over the more *ana* try to straighten.

Ana am like a battered sword

                    that hasn't gotten any less sharp.

Don't leave me!

                    (The sparrow finds the exit suddenly—.)

O you reproachful *wifcynn*:

                    when the men go off

can your witchcraft tell us

              who'll return?

Do you faint

              because they *flet ofgeafon*?

You make everyone weep!

              for the *burston* bodies

of the irreplaceable friends

              of your own youth.

But neither the witches

              nor the necromancers know

what the *aelmihtig* intends.

              Just ask them:

Hwaer cwom the men?

              Hwaer cwom our protectors?

They don't even know

              when the rainstorm will come!

On leftovers *ana* breakfast

        like the spleenish *wulf* the *wéstenes* chase.

He sets out hungry,

        nose in the wind, up the *wulfhleoþu*.

After a luckless trek,

        he *gilleþ*; and gaunt companions answer

(Grayed-out,

        thin as yarrow stalks

Or like bees

        bereaved by a honey thief,

Their mouths agape—

        jaws like hacked tree trunks).

He *gellende* and they *gellende*

        across the desert forum.

He standing and they standing

        blinking sympathy at one another.

He complaining and they complaining
                then mutually turning away—

Comforted.
                Wita sceal geþyldig.

He turning back and they turning back
                in *hæste.*

Earmne anhogan
                hiding his wretchedness.

•

Often *ana* remember a night so cold
                a hunter might even burn his *asca*—

When *ana* stalked the gloam
                with my sidekicks, hunger and misery,

And made *martiras* of women and children
                before the pitch black lifted.

And next day at al-Ghumaysa
                ana overheard this—

"Our hundas *barked and we thought,*
                'Is it a wulf *prowling? a* niht-genge?*'*

But they only growled once
                    then curled back to sleep,

So we thought, 'Is it a sandgrouse
                    or beard-leás?'

But if it was a scinn,
                    his ambush was stunning

But if it was a man . . .
                    what kind of man does this?"

Often, when the dog days
                    bartered mirages for vipers

Ana bared my face to the sun
                    with nothing but my ravaged coat;

My hair wild—
                    long, wild locks—

Years since styled with gel
                    or deloused.

For ana have crisscrossed
                    a printless windsele

And *ana* have drawn

        the wilderness around me

Perched on *windige naessas*

        squatting or standing.

There, fawning goats

        like virgins trailing skirts

Took their afternoon rest with me

        as if *ana* were their billy

With my white legs and long horns

        picking through the mountain pass

Ever receding

        high among the caves.

GLOSSARY

LABID'S "LAST SIMILE"

earn = eagle

gebideo = waiting, alert for

hœgtesse = female seer

morgenceald = morning chill

westen = desert, wasteland

hœste = violence

stela = stealing (along the ground)

eagfleah = whites of his eyes

sweng = strike

eorde = earth

wyrd = destiny

LABID'S "LAMENT"

ana = alone (Anglo-Saxon; also "I" in Arabic)

wyrdstaef = things decreed by fate

gehrorene = decay

wifcynn = womenfolk

flet ofgeafon = die, fly away

burston = broken

aelmihtig = Almighty, God

Hwaer cwom? = where gone?

FROM AL-SHANFARA'S "LAMIYYA"

wulf = wolf

wulfhleoþu = wolf-slopes

gilleþ, gellende = yell, yelling (also used of stringed instruments)

Wita sceal geþyldig = "A wise man must be patient." ("The Wanderer," line 65)

Earmne anhogan = "the solitary wretch" ("The Wanderer," line 40)

asca = spears

martiras = martyrs

hundas = dogs

niht-genge = hyena

beard-leás = hawk

scinn = phantom

windsele = wind-hall; hell

windige naessas = windblown crags

From this balcony the sight lines are clear to the rooftop
    volleyball court of my son's elementary school
(From its mesh cage the kids at PE class raise a right ruckus)
—I look over; is he up there now? No; his is a different period
I'm squeezing some orange halves on a cheap plastic boat with
    a dome like a parliament and teeth at the spout to catch
        seeds and pulp
Dragging a haul of juicing oranges all the way down-campus in
    my bag stitched with the word *Cyprus*
I recall the oranges were mostly on the trees in Cyprus
It was the potato we were about then: the famous Cypriot,
    grown in red dirt and baked "in its jacket," fluffy as a
    buttered cloud . . .
We would pass the fields of red dirt and then a schoolyard and
    wonder what it would be like to be a child raised on an
    island like this
Squat between sun and sea, never an ice age, abounding with
    indigenous flowers evolving freely, without
    extinctions
But, oh yeah—massacres
Barbed wire slicing Nicosia in a crescent ghetto
My grandmother picked potatoes on a collective farm at the
    age of nine, after her father died
But the funny story she told was of having shut herself

inadvertently in the potato cellar while her mother
was ill with pneumonia
The eldest child, she knew that if her mother died as well it
would all be on her shoulders—the infant, the other
children—
And already terrified to begin with, she began bawling
But you know, someone let her out after a few hours
Her mother survived the pneumonia
She survived the potato farm
Then when she was eighteen and working in a hospital kitchen
her supervisor—*Psst!*—opened the pantry and
gestured toward the potatoes, pocketing some in her
overcoat
She was terrified all over again
If she did help herself, their boss, a kind man, would find out
If she didn't help herself, her supervisor would know she knew
She didn't take the potatoes and she didn't get fired, and
decades later she would return to the scene of
demoralization, her version of *The Stalin Years*

The volleyball court has gone silent
The PE teacher, whose name I don't remember, rests his arms
against the ledge and overlooks the street, the campus,
my building, in which I sit, stuck in a thought about
potatoes
He stands there a minute or two, in repose, then turns and
walks away, leaving the scene unpopulated as in some

sketch or exercise by a painter removed from the
north to a Mediterranean Arcadia full of ruins and
cypresses
Oh, it would be an exaggeration to say it's full of ruins here!
More like one of those mythological scenes with youths and
gods in a crowded sky
Bliss Street overflowing with students slowing traffic as they
drift across the road, scooters clustered outside the
gate inscribed with the motto "That life may be lived
more abundantly"
Perfect motto for a university. Perfect
As the fig trees were perfect that grew all into one boxy wreath
round the dry fountain the kids on rented bicycles
circled madly
That survived the civil war by the looks of their thick trunks,
ringed by apartment blocks and antennae raised into a
looming cloud the color of putty. Putty, not *putti*

AFTER SAPPHO (THE VOLCANO)

The clouds mock me with their mimicry
of continental landmasses. Chimerae.

An atmospheric shield of tiny silicates
separates the mother from her sons,
roses from wholesalers.

II

AZURE

It's that wafer ash
set next to the hardy Dutchman's pipe
that reminds me of the unlikely sight
we caught on hotel cable TV:
Al Schön espousing orange wines.
Two decades ago,
he was the school's athlete-Platonist.
And now we're all as louche
and brown around the edges
as this "Baronne Prevost."
The "Julia Child,"
the "Rise 'n' Shine"
— these rosebuds exist
to ornament fulsome christenings.
So it happens today that Azure
is introduced toddling
in a glade of bamboo
topping out at a whisper on the hillside.
"Azure, meet our Gray."
"Gray, Azure."

CANTATA FOR LYNETTE ROBERTS

Lynette, the stars are kerned so far apart—
Through a herniated zodiac I almost see your *waled skylanes,*
    your *shocked Capricorn and Cancer.*
In the hundred and two years since you were born, and the
    sixteen since your heart failed, and the nearly sixty
    since you gave up poetry, it seems we can't navigate by
    the same star chart.
I'd like to think we were fated to work the same coracle: you
    steering with one hand, grasping your corner of the
    seine while I grasp mine; together sweeping the weirs.

Lynette saw the sky made wide-waled corduroy by the flight
    paths of fighter jets.
Corde du roi—"cloth of the king"
("baseless assertion," states the OED).
A fireman from the Midlands NFS said the raids on Swansea
    were worse than on Birmingham, where a ten-year-
    old Roy Fisher gaped at the garden where his cousins
    were slaughtered, and later wrote, *It was like a burst*
    pod filled with clay.

Last night, Lynette, my son thought he saw his father in the
   jumbo jet roaring over Cherryhurst: the weather
   softer, flight paths altered.
Three weeks now his father gone.

●

Insofar as Moses came to in a coracle, it wasn't a Welsh one-off;
　　it wasn't a hapax of vessels.
Insofar as it's kind of a kiddie boat, not a kayak, not the royal
　　barge the Makah sent William Blake, aka Johnny Depp,
　　with into the northern Pacific; not even the Viking
　　ship, its carved prow like an uncial; insofar as it is
　　calico wrapped up in tar, insofar as it is swaddled
　　willow whippets.

●

"Pastoral ding-dong is OUT," Lynette wrote, and no wonder —
   bombs hidden on the glossy knolls.
In the sorrel.
In the tormentil.
I thought she was perhaps the closest I could get to my
   grandmother.
While Lynette was writing "Displaced Persons" —

Neither from the frosted leaf nor from
The grey hard ground could they find
Relief.

— Lydia was migrating, on foot, a thousand miles from Minsk
   to Hannover through the German lines in a different
   tongue.
I only have this one tongue, so I adopt Lynette's epic as a stand-
   in.
She slipped back to childhood in Buenos Aires, garrulous in her
   dying, her children spiriting a Spanish dictionary into
   the facil with them on visits.
I would see again São Paulo, she wrote (my mother would be
   reared there): *the coffee coloured house with its tarmac*
   roof.

I can imagine myself down the same funnel reverting to
   Portuguese and the small pure word-hoard shared
   between child and grandparent: *suja, limpo, bom, mau,*
   com fome, cansado.
Porcaria.
Disgraçada!
Let my children bring the dictionary too.

Lynette was ardent for penillions, and "experimented with a
   poem on Rain by using all words which had long thin
   letters . . ."
Maybe you thrill to such things when English isn't fully
   naturalized.
Hers was a poetry of metals and alloys; air raids they were, ear
   raids . . .

●

I'm not so much crusted with parasangs, or dipped in leagues,
   as fried in miles of a journey resembling the arc
   between Cleo and asp.
The Jacuzzi, on a timer, sank a quarter hour in froth on a fifty-
   degree afternoon.
There were sight lines to windy breakers, heaving palms; we
   floated like epiphytes grown from pond scum, flowers
   of the abyss.

The meliorative air was moist around a gigantic neon cross.
And it's true I found it hard to think of you with the hardness I
thought of myself.
Since it took hundreds and hundreds of dollars of posters to
adorn the walls of that apartment
(Pillsbury Dough kitsch; an art deco cigar teetering on a
stiletto; a wall plaque of a trilobite fossil; photo of the
Sydney Opera House at night; a three-foot geode
with its own spotlight on the end of what looked like a
colonoscope—)
since it took all that to match the bric-a-brac on the beach,
beach that stretched to fill the picture window,
I thought it took many waves to round the facts; an asp to
soften geometric Cleopatra; and that giant cross was
earth's axis extracted—
tendering foliage all over Florida.

•

I'm in the backyard weeding cotyledons.

Croton.

It's spring.

There're larvae noodling in the soil.

"I was rendering a 'whipping' stitch," Lynette wrote, on a silk-
    and-georgette petticoat, the utility of which would be
    tested in Dover, where Keidrych had been called up to
    man the antiaircraft guns.

Had his conscientious objector status been approved on
    appeal, no end to their Arcadia.

Dylan read Rabelais, drank with Keidrych; Lynette sat with
    Caitlin.

Household talk.

Debts.

Children.

Insofar as Croton is rank with cotyledons, insofar as weeding is
    gleeful, insofar as the seedcase still caps their tips, I
    am revising the look of spring on the face of the village.

Insofar as Moses slips through the reeds in his coracle.

With new beaks scissoring the air.

●

Lynette's village, Llanybri, is pronounced *clan-ubree*.
Even the *l*'s turn into *c*'s where modern warfare enters the
    poem as discord: *clinic air.*
Saint *Cadoc* and *curlews* versus *confervoid; cranch-crake* versus
    ceraunic clouds; into euclidian cubes grid air is planed.
Where did she get the nerve?

I pencil in her age where various dates are given: 32 when she
    began *Gods with Stainless Ears;* 36 when she had her
    first child, 37 when she had the second; 39 or 40
    when she divorced.
The nervous breakdown came at 47.
Jehovah's Witness thereafter.
Lynette, if you were here, I'd ask you the one salient question
    for a woman at midpoint:
How not to harden?

•

In Little Sparta, Ian Hamilton Finlay made an image of an Oerlikon gun and inscribed:

To Apollo:
His Music   *His Missiles*   *His Muses*

Like Lynette he observed the swarm-like behavior of fighter jets.

He saw "flame-bearing honey" in the gasoline leaked by immolated warships.

He commemorated the Flower Class Corvette, each a small naval vessel named for a blossom.

Alyssum.

Loosestrife.

The fragility of men in battle.

The *Loosestrife* had eight mounts for each two-pound pom-pom antiaircraft gun.

This was no Arcadian ding-dong either, as the corduroy bridge Finlay built on a stream had a line from Heraclitus on each plank:

That which joins and that which divides is one and the same.

Lynette says: *He, of Bethlehem treading a campaign . . .*

•

It's the nickel in my cheap wedding ring that brings on this
    rash that starts at the corners of my lips.
The ring bought at age twenty-one, paid for with the tips from
    Buddy's Crabs & Ribs.
Which I now paint religiously with clear nail polish on the
    inner band, across the names, the ampersand, where
    the graving bit exposed the nickel.

Out of this hard. Out of this sheet of zinc.
[. . .]
                    We, he and I ran
On to a steel escalator, the white
Electric sun drilling down on the cubed ice;
Our cyanite flesh chilled on aluminum

Rail.

The *tin Madonnas* of warplanes, writ small and annular in
    marriages, hammered out in Lynette's ear raids.

•

My library is wreathed in double staircases climbing to a glass
    dome.
I imagine birds trapped at the top, a cucucurrucued
    curriculum, forming and dissolving figures ad hoc.
Insofar that these are books that were ernes, atom-wise, in
    former eons.

The abbess of Streoneshall, Caedmon's abbess, Hilda, was
    announced to her mother in a pregnancy dream: "a
    most valuable jewel" delivered from under her
    garments.
She wrote one of the books in this aerie, this library wreathed
    in double staircases; lodged also in subdural
    interfaces.
Insofar as we're just pre-ceviche, pre-cadavers-reinterpreting-
    flan, Lynette, let's research articles, with babies at our
    feet: on Welsh architecture, the potato tax, coracles . . .
I see you floating out to sea in your coracle, the spirit of the
    Makah accompanying you as far as the Azores: halfway
    from a kitchen garden in Llanybri, halfway to a *quinta*
    near Buenos Aires.

III

CHAGRIN

I.

SEFERIS, 1950

A provincial town, founded by Phrygians
three thousand years ago; got a hotel.
Elaborate handicrafts much debased
   in the wake of tourism;
but fascinating to watch old men carving.

What does it mean that most of our griefs
are for gourds? Gouged zucchini,
stuffed, lunch laced with mint, arak;
   bedsheet sewn to quilt
(hope the sheets are changed for each new guest).

But on the icon of Jonah, to see inscribed,
"I have been grieving deeply over the gourd
nigh unto death" . . . Some kind of joke
   among a populace
not known for mixing saints and mirth.

The thing I'll never forget:
the town had few automobiles but

all manner of carriages and outmoded coaches
    from the last century,
all over Europe: *landaus, barouches,*

cabriolets, victorias, growlers, broughams,
diligences, equipages, droshkies . . .
Can you see them? Descendants of
    heroic chariots
crepitating, drawn by thin horses.

It's as if they had drifted down the continent
to a point of origin, minus the drivers.
They'd begun their journeys with the dream
    of a homecoming.
I felt a stab of grief for these pumpkins.

II.

You missed your father's homecoming,
missed the obit for Lonesome George
the Galápagos tortoise
    the late-night BBC broadcast,
even as you clutched your turtle pillow.

Highway traffic was sparse but fast,
and greeting us on the airport road:

fountaining LED displays.
    The airport acreage
a kind of fairgrounds after hours.

You missed your father's kiss.
Head at an angle, ten of six,
breathing deeply in your sleep and of it,
    through the very thing
you had longed for and anticipated.

Lonesome George was the last of his kind,
a bachelor through and through;
his name doubled itself—*galápago*
    is Spanish for tortoise,
tortoise English for *galápago*.

Galloping tortoise?—as ungainly a thing
as I could imagine, so when it died,
borne outside its pen in Ecuador
    on a bier, I looked twice
at the turtle pillow you adored.

A *galloping* tortoise—a *pillow turtle*—
the paradoxes of the imagination
held us to no standard, fixed us to no world.
    They froze his tissue
to bring his double back.

But how to clone a lonesome thing?
What his shagreen means to us
isn't just some makeweight to register
    on scales of importance
the slow progress of our feelings.

WINGANDECOIA

Whoso list to hunt it with a camera?
The Carolina parrot is extinct.
Hunted to nothing emerald.

We'll never see its plumage,
which lives only in the image
of psittacines caught on camera

and in Audubon prints;
but what I'd give to hear the *speech* of this prince
of hunted-to-nothing emerald.

Did it lure the colonists inland?
With what speech or song? Gone that song.
A painter on the ship, not camera:

White bade his shallop men sing chaunties
in the dark, but no one emerged
from the forests of maritime emerald.

The birds must have lured them inland:
intelligent Carolina parakeet.
Whoso list to hunt it with a camera,

hunted to nothing emerald?

•

The sea surface the gull patrols
is mollified today. Any painter's
palette amounts to a patois.

It must be this painter's Herculean
labor to limn the sky with cerulean
unruled, which the gull patrols.

It disappears into the myrtle and cordgrass.
Islets of beige, sage, and slate
pass less for a system than a patois.

A value assigned to painters' powers
landed White in New World expeditions.
Better gulls than galleons on patrol.

But now, who's the green governor of this?
Fission of English from its nucleus.
Something more than a patois

says *psittacines. Pot pot chee.* (Seminole
for "smart bird with the Semibabble.")
Gone all but the sea surface the gull patrols

with a palate that determines its patois.

•

The Spanish mustangs that do roam the coast
from here to the border of Virginia
have a chatoyance about their coats.

The chatoyance of spools of thread in a
stall, row upon row of them per the medina.
The Spanish mustangs that do roam the coast

pawn-swapped through history
from the steppes, from Araby
brought the chatoyance of their coats

to where what is aqua turns equine:
the whole world seen through two
descendants of Spanish horses, on this coast,

addorsed on a dune, backlit by sunset:
Foaming necks rising from the Atlantic,
chatoyance of beach grass like lined coats;

reeds and phragmites a kind of mane.
Legatees of the Spanish main,
the mustangs that do sheen the coast

with chatoyance of spools in their coats.

•

That they survived the centuries is a kind of marvel
—so much gone, all our study is fossils:
What's gone becomes our greatest marvel.

Once, among a cabinet of curiosities,
a nobleman displayed a child mummy.
That it survived the centuries was a kind of marvel.

For us there's little magic that remains
except as what has managed to escape us:
What is gone becomes our greatest marvel.

There was *bells from Henry VIII's fool*;
also, *fireflies from Virginia*.
That fireflies survive is a kind of marvel.

A species—a plant will do—newly discovered
not to be extinct after all, makes headlines.
What's gone becomes our greatest marvel.

Gone Raleigh's colony, gone Wyatt's sonnet,
gone *pot pot chee*, the Carolina parrot.
Anything that survives the centuries is a kind of marvel

though what's gone becomes our greatest marvel.

●

I am jealous of the *hoc est corpus*
with which a priest transubstantiates a wafer.
Not what's written in horoscopes.

Take the one-and-a-half whorl
that springs from a conch's seedcase.
I am jealous of the *hoc est corpus*.

John Dee brought back black ore
from his Arctic explorations.
In Mortlake, he cast horoscopes.

He brought back Nugumiut: Calichoughe,
who died, and a mother and child too.
His proof of their existence: *hoc est corpus*.

Egnock and Nutioc preserved in miniature,
not by Dee but by the artist-governor of Virginia.
What use have artists for horoscopes?

Watercolors rendered with white knuckles
the delicacy of the mother-daughter nucleus.
I am jealous of his *hoc est corpus*,

not whorl-counting horoscopes.

•

Governance from a distance, like a star—
Sir "Water" Raleigh (per his accent)
whose mistress gasped *swisser swatter!*

swisser swatter! massaged against a tree.
He sent his people to the *pot pot chee*
and governed from a distance, like a star.

But the psittacines are silent when
—*whoso list to hunt*—a silver cup is gone.
Up against a wall, *swisser swatter,*

Native Aquascogoc is set on fire.
A silver (*Communion!*) cup. Gone the communion:
thanks to governance from a star.

But *stars may fall, nay they must fall
when they trouble the sphere wherein they abide.*
Down upon a block, *swisser swatter,*

they chopped his head. Gone that language,
in truth: all of its pomp and plumage:
governance from a distance, like a star,

and down against the block, *swisser swatter.*

•

It feels emeritus:
As if asterisking alternate endings to this history,
the ghost crab emerges

along a rumpled smorgasbord.
An octave in perfect consonance with itself.
It feels emeritus:

For its presentation
as a ripple in the vision
it is dubbed ghost, when dusk emerges.

Meanwhile, a whole armada lies offshore.
Here, here, writ the mirrored feet:
It feels emeritus.

Croatoans claimed a ship plied the coast,
searching for the settlers,
ghostly as the crab when it emerges.

Sightings inland. Daughter, granddaughter gone.
Landscape of sage, fawn hair.
It feels emeritus—the very name, the stars—

when, at dusk, a ghost crab emerges.

●

Named for a queen under the sign of Virgo:
the painter's New World grandchild.
In truth, that language is gone.

Legend has it she was turned long ago
into a deer—*whoso list to hunt*—
though named for a queen under the sign of Virgo.

Her dying word was *Dare*, they swear,
when the arrow turned her back into a maid.
In truth, that language is gone.

Under the governance of a poet and a painter,
the experiment faltered.
But the terrain was the queen's, under the sign of Virgo.

Their word and their witness never amounted
to a whorl and a half of what the court commanded.
In truth, their language is gone.

Swisser swatter. Pot pot chee. Hoc est corpus.
I send you postcards from Wingandecoia
under the jurisdiction of a queen, Virgo;

in truth my language gone.

ANGÉLIQUE

Supercumulonimbus
storming over downtown on a Sunday
—pop. *poof.*
St. John's Passion in progress.

First performed on this continent
in Bethlehem, Pennsylvania, in 1888.
In 1981, Ursuline nuns from Poland
rained down blows

on sixth-grade boys in Pennsylvania.
The look of a boy's bent back in its white button-down . . .
While the libretto promised us
the bent back of the scapegoat

is the covenantal *regenbogen,*
rising like a vinegar swab on a hyssop branch
was a long-necked *angélique.*
Herr Jesu Christ, erhöre mich . . .

It's a heresy to think
that because such music came from humans,
humans must be equally perfectible.
But to have an afterlife as melody

(pop. *poof*) I submit,
is better than imagining (Whitman) myself a lilac,
or atoms in the perpetual billows
of the reactors at Limerick.

REASON, LOVE, CONTROL

An oneirogenic agent,
   the *Silene*,
will give you vivid dreams
   or so a butterfly larva,
like the Grey Chi, which feeds on it,
   could tell you. I am a scientist
with an eldritch proboscis
   scouring the Siberian permafrost
   for one lupine or campion germ
in a squirrel's Pleistocene stash.
   A sea-Adam, a sea-Eve,
cast out some time ago
   once looked at their hands
and feet in astonishment.
   Now fish now mammal now both,
thinks the breaching dolphin,
   and in that instant,
death's opacity
   fills ampoules of shrimp
for our table.
   The here-and-now crowns
shelves of rocks, tablets,
   bones and papyrus
stamped with a hermetic style

it would take a more original
organ to decode, as to its low-slung Eden
   our dolphin returns with a lunge.
Against your mother's viscera,
   you felt the tide fall
toward the foreshore.
   Your eyes you inherited
from the stigma of a photosynthetic
   chloroplast. Your nose
is but the pointed anterior end
   of the first flagellate presenting polarity;
your mouth the elaboration
   of the oral depression
formed in response to the propulsion
   of the anterior flagellum.
This inherited equipment
   suggests that nothing living,
not even seaweed, deserves contempt
   so long as the output
makes good the wastage.
   Love sets its crampons
in decaying somata
as a fiddlehead stakes its sylvan citation
   on shot-over land.
We're sitting in my sister's house.
   We could go to the aquarium, she says.
Medusozoan nerve nets.

Pterophyllum altum
so laterally compressed
   that, like impending disaster,
it disappears when regarded head-on —
   right under my nose
my father diagnosed.
   In that smoothing out
of every wrinkle in his brain,
   a transfer of fretwork to my face.
So, say he is becoming more baby
   as I become evidence of origami
folded and refolded along a learning curve.
   Etiology speculative —
Exposure to solvents, benzene,
   petroleum products.
Hypertension, loss of axons,
   cerebral infarction.
I would have been kinder,
   had I known
the day he dismantled my car
   that widespread white matter
lesions and hemorrhage
   were subtly but inexorably
leading to impaired executive functions
   and processing speed.
I remember that November day
   in Pennsylvania —

mixing in every kind of sky,
and prying the leaves off one by one
  with as many pincer grips
as a gale can chopstick.
  Coolly the bodies of experts,
the professional committees,
  hone their vocab to tweezers.
And I love it too. I love how it controls
  my breathing—*subcortical, ischemic*—
for we life-forms are evolving
  only toward more feeling.

•

•

•

NOTES

Various poems in this book were midwifed by my reading. A selected bibliography would include Aristotle's treatises "On the Naming and Situation of the Winds" and "On Marvelous Things Heard"; Colin Thubron's *Journey into Cyprus*; Roberto Calasso's *Literature and the Gods*; Philip Mansel's *Levant*; Henry Miller's *The Colossus at Maroussi*; George Seferis's journals; *Early Arabic Poetry*, ed. Alan Jones; *The Homeric Hymns*, Pindar, Homer, and Cavafy. "Wingandecoia" was informed by my reading of *Roanoke*, by Lee Miller.

ACKNOWLEDGMENTS

Thanks to the editors of these journals for first publishing the following poems:

Cerise Press: "Naiad Math"
London Review of Books: "Civilization"
The Nation: "After Sappho (The Volcano)," "Azure," "Cicadas"
The New Yorker: "Bliss Street"
The Paris Review: "Alexander's Naming of the Winds," "Lamiyya," "Wingandecoia"
Parnassus: "Chagrin"
Plume: "Hurricane: Hera," "Squall: Echo"
Poetry: "Cantata for Lynette Roberts," "The Grind," "Last Simile," "Stabile," "Symphonic Expanse"
Port Magazine: "Flashflood: Arethusa"
Smartish Pace: "The Med"
The Southern Review: "The Heliopolitan"

Thanks to the editorial staff at *Poetry* magazine for the Frederick Bock Prize for "Cantata for Lynette Roberts."

I'm grateful to John McNamara at the University of Houston for helping me with Anglo-Saxon (any errors are, of course, mine). Thanks to the wonderful people who made my year in Beirut one of the most memorable experiences of my life. And thanks to my husband, Steven McNamara, for dragging me around the world against my will. It's good for poetry.

Printed in the USA
CPSIA information can be obtained
at www.ICGtesting.com
LVHW091147150724
785511LV00005B/598